D1531275

Grandmother's
Household
Hints

Written by Marian Hoffman

AVENEL
New York

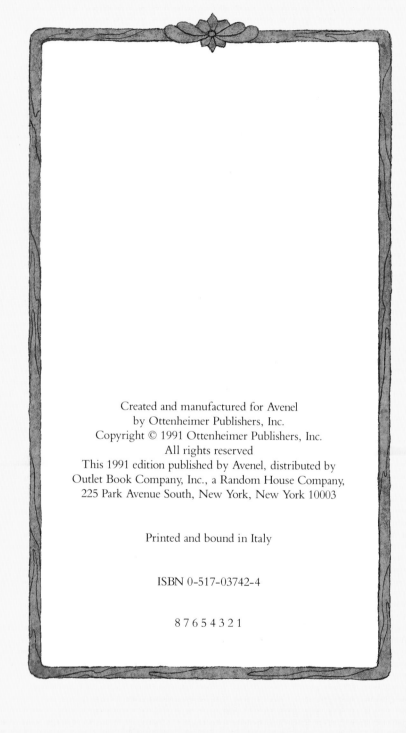

Created and manufactured for Avenel
by Ottenheimer Publishers, Inc.
Copyright © 1991 Ottenheimer Publishers, Inc.
This 1991 edition published by Avenel, distributed by
Outlet Book Company, Inc., a Random House Company,
225 Park Avenue South, New York, New York 10003

Printed and bound in Italy

ISBN 0-517-03742-4

8 7 6 5 4 3 2 1

Contents

Good Scents

You can add a pleasant scent to your clothes closet with a citrus pomander. Pomanders can also be stored in a closed drawer or cabinet, or hung in cupboards or from ceiling beams. I like to decorate my pomanders with pretty satin or velvet ribbons and display them in bowls on the window sill.

Citrus Pomander

1 orange, lemon, grapefruit, or lime
About 25 whole cloves
1 1/2 teaspoons orris root powder
1 1/2 teaspoons ground cinnamon

Stud the fruit with the cloves. If the cloves break while trying to pierce the rind, make small holes with a toothpick first. Combine the orris root powder and cinnamon. Roll the clove-studded fruit in the mixture. Wrap in tissue paper and store for 2 to 3 weeks in a warm, dry, dark place. Decorate with embroidered or satin ribbons.

Floral Pomanders

Make floral pomanders by covering a ball of dry florist's foam with a rubber-based glue and rolling the foam in scented dried flowers and spices. Decorate with satin or embroidered ribbon.

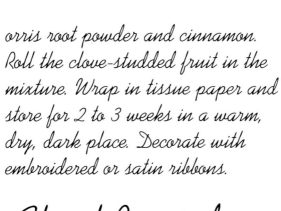

Dried Flowers

I fill my house with fragrant bunches of dried flowers to see me through the dull winter months, some hanging in swags from the windows, some arranged in jars, and others simply laid in a basket and displayed on the mahogany sideboard in my dining room.

To dry flowers, I first strip off all the leaves from the stems. With old nylons, I fasten them in bunches containing no more than 10 flowers each and hang them upside down in a dark, dry place for a week to 10 days.

This is a good method for drying delicate flowers that might break when air dried. Combine 5 cups white cornmeal with 1½ cups

borax. Place the mixture in the bottom of a shoe box to a depth of 1 inch. Make a shallow depression in the mixture and carefully set the flower into it face up. Sprinkle the cornmeal-borax mixture over the flower until the entire blossom is covered. The flower should be covered by at least 1 inch of the cornstarch-borax mixture. Set aside for 6 to 10 days.

When the flowers are dried, I fill a container with 4 inches of sand, wire the dried flower stems and insert them into the sand. The dried flowers must not be kept in a humid room or the flowers will wilt.

Spray dried flower arrangements with hair spray to preserve them.

Cut Flowers

My mother was always the great flower arranger in our family. She had a most impressive garden and the flowers kept our house filled with wonderful colors and fragrances throughout the spring and summer. Visitors to our house were greeted by the scent of fresh flowers when they came through the front door.

There was a large glass bowl in the entrance hall. Its bottom was thickly covered with small, colorful pebbles to serve as support for the flower stems and add a festive touch to the arrangement.

Try some of these to preserve your cut flowers:

Add aspirin tablets to the water

Add pennies to the water

Add ice cubes to the water

Add 1 teaspoon of vinegar and 1 teaspoon of sugar for each pint of water used.

Add weak tea to the water

Add a thin slice of soap to the water

Add 1 teaspoon of salt to the water

Potpourri

There's something warm and welcoming about a house filled with good smells. To lend fragrance to the house wrap bunches of herbs together with twine and hang them in the kitchen to lend fragrance to the house.

To release the natural scent of herb potpourri, I sometimes place the potpourri in boiling water and continue to boil it until the house is filled with fragrance. I also enjoy storing pretty guest soaps in baskets filled with potpourri, so that the soaps absorb the scents.

Try this potpourri recipe:
1 teaspoon cinnamon powder
1/2 oz. orris root powder
2 drops rose oil

½ drop patchouli oil
1 drop lavender oil
2 cups dried rose petals
½ oz. lavender
1 oz. lemon verbena

Place the cinnamon and the orris root powder in a small bowl. Add the rose, lavender and patchouli oils, mixing well. Combine the rose petals, lavender, and lemon verbena in a separate bowl. Combine the 2 mixtures, mixing together thoroughly. Place in an airtight container and leave in a dark place for 6 weeks. Shake the container once every day for the first week.

Potpourri can be used to make scented sachets, and for placing in drawers to scent clothing, stationery, or linens.

Herb Window Boxes

While many herbs are grown for seasoning, others are grown primarily for their fragrance. An indoor herb garden lends a subtle, pleasing scent to the room. Small pots of herbs can be placed along the window sill, on brackets attached to the side of the window frame, or on glass shelves across the window. Most herbs need a sunny window. Use a good sandy loam to which some compost has been added. Don't let the herbs dry out, but don't over water, mist them once a week.

The leaves of fragrant herbs can be floated in finger bowls for a

pleasing scent at the dinner table.
I particularly like using rose gera-
nium, lemon verbena, and lemon
balm leaves.

The following fragrant herbs do
well indoors:

Sweet basil	Scented geraniums
Lemon Balm	Lemon Verbena
Savory	Sweet Woodruff
Thyme	

Deodorizing Your House

My favorite trick is to throw dried orange and lemon rinds into the fire in my fireplace, to fill my house with a delicious, spicy scent.

A simple way to clear the air is to place partially filled bowls of baking soda or white vinegar inconspicuously around the room. I find this particularly useful when I'm having company and want to prevent the room from smelling of stale cigarette smoke.

To make my favorite homemade deodorizer, place 4 drops wintergreen oil on a cotton ball. Place the scented cotton ball in an open container. The fresh scent will last for

several months. Wintergreen oil can be purchased at a drug store.

Sometimes, after repeated washing, my glass jars and vases still have a lingering smell. I restore their freshness by filling the containers with baking soda dissolved in cold water. I then wash the containers in hot, soapy water and rinse.

My baking soda solution also removes smells from dishcloths, sponges, and towels. Baking soda is a wonderful deodorizer. Place an opened box of baking soda in the refrigerator to absorb odors and replace it every 2 months. Try dipping a small cotton ball in vanilla and placing it on a saucer in the refrigerator.

Candles

I always keep a supply of bayberry candles on hand to use throughout the year to perfume my house. I light the candles, let them burn for a few minutes, then blow them out. The smoke fills the house with a pleasing, slightly spicy fragrance.

To make your own scented candles, melt the ends of used candles in a double boiler. Add whole cloves, or other spices of your choice. Pour the melted wax into molds with wicks. Use the scented candles as air fresheners.

Lightly spray your favorite cologne on some candles. When the candles are burned, the fragrance of the cologne will spread throughout the room.

Candles also make an attractive decoration for the room and set an inviting mood. To keep candles clean, dip a cloth in alcohol and wipe the candle lightly.

Candles become dripless when soaked in salt water. For each candle, dissolve 2 tablespoons of salt in water to cover the candles. Soak the candles for 15 minutes.

Sparkling Tips

I find baking soda to be indispensable. I use it to deodorize my refrigerator and carpets.

Baking soda is great for cleaning chrome, porcelain, and pots and pans. The best homemade all-purpose cleanser I've found also is made with baking soda:

1/8 cup baking soda
1/4 cup white vinegar
1/2 cup household ammonia
1 gallon warm water

Add the baking soda, vinegar, and ammonia to the water, mixing well. Use less water for a stronger solution.

Borax is also a handy item to have for household cleaning jobs.

To clean dirty wallpaper, you can dip a cloth into powdered borax and rub it over the soiled areas. A mixture of ¼ cup borax and 1 teaspoon ammonia mixed in ½ gallon water makes a great cleaner that is especially effective for cleaning painted walls. Using a soft sponge, wash the walls from the bottom up.

You don't need special cleaning solutions to remove the smudges, grease, and dirt spots that seem to spontaneously appear on walls and other surfaces. Rubbing smudges with a piece of stale bread will also do the trick. Remove grease spots by rubbing a small amount of talcum powder over the spots with a powder puff until all the grease is absorbed.

Soap

Armed with a bar of soap, I feel equipped to handle virtually all household needs.

Soap cleans and scents. It greases screws and nails, lubricates stuck drawers, doors, and windows, stops runs in nylon stockings, prevents metal surfaces from rusting, and helps saw blades move easily.

Soap comes in different varieties, and has different cleaning purposes. Jelly soap has a variety of uses, including washing dishes and laundry.

Try this jelly soap recipe:
3 tablespoons white soap flakes
1 cup boiling water
2 teaspoons borax

Dissolve the soap in the boiling

water. Stir in the borax. You can also make a jelly soap that is good for hand washable laundry by dropping leftover soap slivers into a cold-cream jar. Add enough boiling water to form a jelly. Leftover soap slivers can also be made into a wonderful liquid soap. Place them in your blender with some water and process until creamy. Pour into plastic squeeze bottles and place by the sink.

Polishing
Furniture

My furniture is a mingling of family treasures—an oak blanket chest, a few Queen Anne chairs, and the mahogany dining room set I bought when I got married.

An old-time cleaning method is to use weak tea. Dip a cloth in the cooled tea and rub the furniture; then wipe it dry with a clean cloth.

Here is a special polish for old oak pieces:

Place 1 pint beer, 1/2 tablespoon sugar, and 1 tablespoon beeswax in a saucepan and bring to a boil. Remove from heat and cool. Wipe the polish onto the wood with a clean cloth. Let dry, then polish with a chamois cloth.

To polish mahogany, mix 1 cup of vinegar and 1 cup of warm water together. Apply and buff to a shine with a soft cloth.

Furniture can also be cleaned and polished by lightly applying mayonnaise with a soft, clean cloth.

I love giving my furniture a shine after polishing by sprinkling on a little cornstarch. I then rub with a clean cloth until glossy.

Add a spoonful of lemon oil to the rinse cycle when you wash your dust clothes to keep them lightly oiled.

Try wearing a pair of old socks like gloves and dampening them with furniture polish. Your polishing will be finished in half the usual time!

Polishing Metals

With the help of some common household items, you can get all the metal items in your house gleaming again.

My old friend baking soda is indispensable as a metal polish. To clean silver, I make a paste by mixing baking soda with a little water. Using a clean cloth, I rub the mixture into the silver, rinse in warm water, and dry well—and the silver is shining again!

Sprinkle baking soda on a slice of lemon. It makes a great cleaner for brass and copper.

Your toothpaste also makes an effective silver polish. After applying, wash the object in warm soap suds, rinse, and dry well.

The next time your milk goes sour, don't throw it away. Soak your silver overnight in a pan of the sour milk or buttermilk. Rinse with cold water and dry well.

Hot sour milk or buttermilk also effectively polishes brass and copper. Worcestershire sauce makes a good brass polish, as does lemon juice.

Immaculate Laundry

If your laundry never looks as clean and bright as you would like, household products such as vinegar, ammonia, and baking soda will save the day.

Clean laundry starts with a clean washer. Once a month, fill the washer with warm water. Add 1 cup of white vinegar and run through the entire cycle. This removes any soap scum and mineral deposits that build up from laundry detergents or soap.

White vinegar is also useful when washing clothes by machine or hand because it dissolves the alkalines in soaps and detergents. Add 1 cup of vinegar to the rinse cycle for clean, fresh smelling clothes, or add it to the water when hand washing delicate clothing. Baking soda is a gentle cleanser for hand-washable fabrics.

Adding vinegar to the rinse cycle will also eliminate any lint on your clothing. Add ½ cup of baking soda to the wash water to make your clothes come out soft and fresh-smelling.

Ammonia is a handy product for cleaning laundry. Adding ½ cup of household ammonia to the wash water will clean even the dirtiest work clothes.

Even with repeated washing and bleaching, I had never been able to get white socks really white again until I placed a slice of lemon in a pot of boiling water and boiled the socks for several minutes.

Cleaning Glass & Crystal

Clean glass invites sunlight into the room to sparkle merrily. It's amazing how simply cleaning the crystal goblets displayed in my corner cabinet makes my entire dining room brighter.

To clean cut glass, I depend again on baking soda. I sprinkle the baking soda on a damp cloth and rub the glass gently. Then I rinse the glass with clear, hot water and dry it.

I also wash crystal in 1 cup of vinegar mixed with 3 cups of warm water and let it air dry.

Lemon juice makes a good glass cleaner; just apply to the glass and dry with a soft cloth. Mix 1

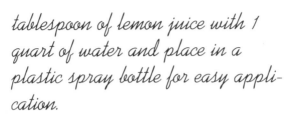

tablespoon of lemon juice with 1
quart of water and place in a
plastic spray bottle for easy appli-
cation.

Dissolving 2 tablespoons of borax
in 3 cups of water also makes an
effective glass cleaner. Remember
never to wash your windows when
the sun is shining right on them,
or the glass cleaners will dry too
fast and streak.

Cleaning the Kitchen and Bathroom

I find borax useful to clean, deodorize, and disinfect both rooms. Add ½ cup of borax to 1 gallon of hot water, and apply with a clean sponge.

Club soda can also be used to clean and shine appliances and countertops.

To clean the grout between kitchen and bathroom tiles, use a paste made of 3 parts baking soda to 1 part warm water to scrub the tile. If the grout becomes so dirty that nothing seems to help, mix ½ cup laundry bleach with 1 quart of warm water and scrub into the

grout with an old toothbrush. Let it set for several minutes, then rinse thoroughly.

The following is a ceramic tile cleaner that I use once a week in my bathroom and kitchen:

¹/₈ cup baking soda
¹/₄ cup white vinegar
¹/₂ cup household ammonia
¹/₂ gallon warm water

Combine the baking soda, vinegar, and ammonia. Add the water, stirring, until the baking soda dissolves. Scrub the mixture onto the tiles with a sponge or brush. Rinse well.

Wooden kitchen surfaces can be cleaned with a baking soda and water paste, or by rubbing half a cut lemon over the wood, rinsing, and drying. Sprinkle the wood with salt to absorb moisture.

Spotless Living

After a Thanksgiving gathering at my house, I discovered white stains from wet glasses on my mahogany table. Fortunately, I remembered a technique that works particularly well on mahogany furniture. Spread a thick coating of petroleum jelly or mayonnaise over the white spot, let it sit for 48 hours, then wipe it off. The stain will vanish. Sure enough, it worked for me and the table is as good as new!

Here are some other dandy tricks for removing the stains left by water or hot dishes: Sprinkle the stains with salt, then rub gently with a cloth dipped in vegetable shortening. When the stain is gone, wash the surface and wax.

Dampen a piece of flannel with peppermint essence or camphor spirits and rub lightly over the stain. Cover with furniture polish.

Make an abrasive by forming a paste with a mixture of cigarette or fireplace ashes and olive or mineral oil. Apply gently to the spot, let stand a few minutes, and buff dry.

Removing Fabric Stains

As a rule, greasy stains can be removed by rubbing liquid detergent into the stain, then rinsing with hot water. Nongreasy stains can be soaked in cool water overnight; then work a detergent into the stain and rinse.

Try these methods to remove common stains:

Blood: Soak in cold water overnight, then wash with soap and warm water. Or, cover the stain with meat tenderizer, add just enough cold water to make a paste and let it set for 30 minutes. Sponge with cool water.

Candle Wax: Place the stained

fabric between paper towels and press with an iron.

Chewing Gum: Press ice cubes against the gum, or chill the garment until the gum becomes brittle, then scrape it away. Gum can also be removed by soaking the fabric in white vinegar or rubbing it with egg white before washing.

Chocolate: Wet the stained area, then rub in borax soap powder. Roll up and set aside for 15 minutes. Scrub with a brush.

Cosmetics: Apply liquid detergent to the stain and work it in until the outline of the stain vanishes.

Food Grease: Rub soap into the stain and soak in warm water.

Ink: Place rubbing alcohol on the stain before laundering or spray the stain with hair spray.

Removing Carpet Stains

I'll never forget when my neighbor came over to admire my new carpet and promptly spilled a cup of coffee on it. I immediately poured club soda on the stain, let it set for a few seconds, and gently sponged it up.

Club soda is also effective for removing alcohol, blood, and pet stains from carpet. Shaving cream, toothpaste, and glass cleaner also are fantastic stain removers; just apply to the spot and wash off with water. The trick is to act fast in order to remove stains before they set.

If a stain has set, work a mixture of 2 tablespoons detergent, 1 quart warm water, and 3 tablespoons vinegar into the carpet, then blot dry.

Brush grease or gravy stains with baking soda or cornmeal, leave overnight, and vacuum.

Combine 1 cup starch and just enough buttermilk to make a paste. Spread the paste over the stain and let it dry before rubbing off.

Removing Stains from Cooking and Servingware

If coffee stains are in the hairline cracks in the glaze of old china cups, make a paste of baking soda and water. Brush the paste on the stained area and let stand for an hour before washing with soap and water. This paste also works well on stains in plastic cups.

Wet stained cups with vinegar, then dip a damp cloth in salt and rub the coffee or tea stains away.

The stains in a glass coffee maker will disappear if you fill it with water, add 1 teaspoon of baking soda and 1 teaspoon of soap pow-

der. Bring the water to a boil and simmer for 10 minutes; rinse with clean water.

To remove the sediment from a tea kettle, mix 1½ cups of apple cider vinegar, 1½ cups of water, and 3 tablespoons of salt together in the kettle and boil for 15 minutes. Set aside overnight, then rinse well.

Stains on a non-stick pan can be removed by boiling 2 tablespoons of baking soda and 1 cup of water in the pan for 15 minutes. Rinse, dry, and coat the pan with vegetable oil.

Sprinkle burnt food with baking soda and a little water. Let sit for a few hours before rinsing.

Removing Stains from Porcelain Appliances

Our old bathroom had a lot of charm with its pedestal sink and claw-foot tub. But the discolored and stained porcelain never looked clean.

The old stains responded well to a homemade cleaner made from a bar of naphtha soap: Shave one 6½ ounce bar of naphtha soap into a 2-gallon bucket filled with hot water. Add ½ cup mineral spirits, stirring until the soap has dissolved. Brush the mixture onto the porcelain, and rinse well.

Light stains on porcelain appliances often disappear after being rubbed with a cut lemon. For darker stains, try scrubbing on a paste made of 3 parts cream of tartar to 1 part hydrogen peroxide.

Baking soda effectively removes many stains from porcelain. Dip a damp cloth into the baking soda and rub over the stains until clean. Rinse well.

Removing Mildew

In warm, humid environments mildew is frequently a problem. To remove mildew from shower curtains, wash with baking soda, then rub with lemon juice. Soaking shower curtains in salt water before hanging them helps prevent mildew from forming.

If mildew grows on clothing or curtains, brush off what you can outside to prevent scattering the spores in the house. Wash with chlorine bleach or hydrogen peroxide, depending on the fabric. Permanent press, double knit fabrics, and white fabrics should be soaked in lemon juice, then rubbed with salt and placed in the sun to bleach.

To remove mildew from linens, soak them for a few minutes in sour milk and hang to dry in the sun.

The best way to fight mildew is to prevent it from forming in the first place. Keep areas clean and dry. Try using a solution of borax and water to clean areas prone to mildew. Don't leave wet or damp fabrics lying around. Keep rooms well ventilated and allow room for air to circulate behind furniture placed against the wall. Use air conditioners and dehumidifiers to remove excess moisture from your home. Placing a piece of charcoal in your bookcases can help to absorb dampness there.

The Essential Tools

There seem to be an endless number of small jobs to do around the house. Having a well-organized tool collection at your disposal makes fix-it jobs a lot easier to handle. I recommend keeping the following basic tools in your tool kit:

1 claw hammer

1 utility knife

1 hand saw

1 hack saw

1 tape measure

1 electric drill and bits

1 combination square

1 level

1 each 4-inch flat-blade & 6-inch flat-blade screwdriver

1 6-inch Phillips screwdriver
1 slip-joint pliers
1 8-inch adjustable wrench
1 file
1 awl
1½-inch wood chisel

Keep your tools well oiled to keep them from rusting. If rust spots do appear, rub the rust off with steel wool soaked with lubricating oil.

Squeaks

I've always felt that part of the charm of old houses is their idiosyncracies—the walls are never straight and the floorboards always creak.

There is a certain point, however, where what used to seem charming becomes merely annoying. Noisy floorboards frequently can be silenced by pouring hot liquid soap into the cracks between the boards causing the trouble.

I've also had some success stopping floors from squeaking by squirting graphite or talc into the cracks between the boards. Graphite, which is used to lubricate locks, is readily available in hardware stores.

Squeaky hinges can also grate on your nerves. Try spraying the offending hinge with nonstick vegetable spray. If your inside doors continue squeaking, remove the hinge pins, one at a time, and rub them well with a soft lead pencil.

If it's your bed springs that are squeaking annoyingly, spritz them with spray wax. When the squeak is caused by the springs rubbing against the bed frame, padding the frame with small pieces of sponge will solve the problem.

Sometimes it's a piece of furniture that is driving you crazy with its squeaking. Try dropping a small amount of melted paraffin into its joints to silence the squeaking.

Sticking Doors, Drawers, & Windows

I often have a problem in damp weather with my doors, dresser drawers, and windows sticking. Brushing a mixture of 2 parts oil and 1 part turpentine on the drawer runners, door, window frame, and window grooves helps prevent this problem.

The drawers of our pine dresser usually stick in damp weather because the wood swells. When this happens to any drawer, remove it and wipe off any dust. Rub the runners and the edges of the drawer with candle wax or a moistened bar of soap.

Soap is also an effective antidote for stuck doors and windows. On doors, rub the soap where the door is scraping.

To loosen windows, rub the soap in the jambs and stop strips. If dampness has swollen the window sash so that it sticks, try forcing wax in between the sash and stop strips. If this doesn't help, remove the sash and plane down the area that sticks.

Sprucing Up Brooms & Paint Brushes

The best way to clean a broom is to soak it in a bucket filled with hot water, a little ammonia, and soap suds. Rinse well and let it dry, upended on the broomstick before storing it away.

Your old paint brushes, too, can be restored to their former shape and texture. Stiff and dry brushes can be softened by being placed in a pot of boiling vinegar for a few minutes, then cleaned with hot soapy water.

Here's my favorite formula for cleaning and softening old paint brushes:

2 tablespoons salt
½ cup kerosene
1 quart warm water

Combine the salt, kerosene, and water in a bucket. Place the brushes in the mixture and soak for 2 hours. Remove and wipe with a clean cloth.

If your paintbrushes have lost their shape and no longer can be used efficiently, try soaking the bristles in a water-soluble glue for several minutes. Reshape the brush and let dry. Rub the bristle tips over a piece of coarse sandpaper until they are the desired shape.

Dip the brush in hot water to remove the glue. After you've washed your brushes, try placing a fabric softener in the final rinse water. This will help keep the brushes soft and flexible.

Wobbly Chair & Table Legs

I spent months eating dinner while sitting on a chair that wobbled to and fro throughout the meal before I finally became fed up and decided to do away with the wobbly chair leg once and for all.

A good way to fix chairs or tables that wobble because of a short leg is to lengthen the short leg with wood putty. Place a piece of waxed paper on the floor and squeeze a small amount of wood putty onto the paper. Set the shorter leg on the putty, pushing it down until the chair or table is sitting level. Let the putty dry completely before trimming off any excess with a knife. File and sand the putty until smooth. Paint or stain the putty to match the rest of the chair or table.

If the chair or table wobbles because one leg is loose, remove the loose leg and wrap the joining end with a small strip of nylon hose or thread. Apply glue, then press into position and let dry.

Furniture Scratches & Nicks

My grandson dropped a heavy ashtray on my coffee table, causing a sizable dent. I tried a trick that a neighbor had once shown me.

First I placed a damp cloth over the dent, then I put a bottle cap on top of the cloth, centered over the dent. I rested a warm iron on top of the bottle cap for a few minutes. I repeated this procedure several times, which caused the wood fibers in the dent to swell, making the dent much less apparent.

When painted furniture gets chips or nicks in it, I rub a wax crayon that matches the paint color

over the chipped area. This fills in the spot and camouflages the damage.

Try some of the these tricks, depending on the type of wood that has been scratched:

For scratches on walnut, shell a fresh, unsalted walnut or pecan. Break the nut in half and rub over the scratch with the broken side until it blends with the finish. Wipe lightly with a clean cloth.

For scratches on maple, mix 1 tablespoon of iodine with 1 tablespoon of denatured alcohol. Use a cotton swab to apply the mixture onto the scratch. Let dry, then wax and buff.

For scratches on mahogany, rub with a dark brown crayon or buff with brown paste wax.

Index

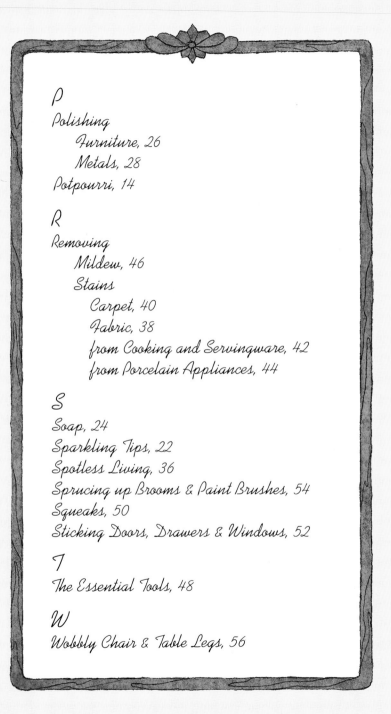